BARDEN'S PEOPLE

A series of selected
interviews by
Westmorland Gazette
feature writer
KAREN BARDEN

First printed:
1994

ISBN:
0-902272-91-8

Published by:
Westmorland Gazette Newspapers, 22 Stricklandgate, Kendal,
Cumbria LA9 4NE.

Cover photograph:
Morecambe Bay fisherman Jack Manning on the sands of the bay, by
Gazette chief photographer Mike Barker.

Printed by:
Miller Turner Printers Ltd, Beezon Road, Kendal, Cumbria LA9 6BS

3-95

THE AUTHOR: Karen Barden

Acknowledgement

WHEN Westmorland Gazette Newspapers launched its mid-week Lakes Leader in March, 1987, editor John Lannaghan asked me to write a women's page. I met many remarkable characters, but I was missing out on too many gems - of the masculine gender.

Barden File in the Leader gave way to Barden's People in the Gazette in January, 1991, and from that time I have been inspired by a continuous stream of heroes. Not necessarily famous, not even infamous, just every day folk who have made their mark.

I am eternally grateful to all those candid, charismatic people to whom my weekly page belongs.

In selecting the pieces for this book and compiling the chapters I have matched personalities under appropriate headings.

I would like to pay tribute to Westmorland Gazette staff photographers Mike Barker and Steve Barber for the pictures in this book and for the work they and Paul Bramham produce week by week for my page.

KB

Dedication

TO THE two Gazette JLs and Jess for making this book happen.

3

Preface

I ALWAYS knew Karen Barden's page was a popular feature of The Westmorland Gazette.

I didn't realise how popular until a regular reader sent us a postcard saying he had just met a man in the Hebrides who subscribed to the Gazette every week just to read Barden's People.

So that set us thinking.

Why not pull together some of her favourite interviews and reproduce them in book form....?

This is the highly enjoyable result.

John Lannaghan
Editor
Westmorland Gazette
October 1994

Contents

Photographs

1

The agony and the ecstasy

John Tovey: A man of good taste

Published May 3, 1991

A canny lass, was his grandmother. She showed him what good cooking was all about and died in his arms before she could see the pinnacle of his success. But she knows, said John Tovey, owner of Windermere's Miller Howe hotel, master chef, writer, broadcaster, household name.

"She has never left me. I continually feel her at my side."

In a childhood of deprivation and regular beatings - there was no Esther Rantzen then - it was grandmother who became young John's rock, his shelter and his haven.

He spent his early years at her side in the back streets of Barrow-in-Furness. Money was scarce, hard-earned. Life a carbon copy of Catherine Cookson's novels.

Every day Gran cooked until she filled an enormous basket of food, which she would hike down to Vickers' shipyard to sell to workers for dinner bait.

On the way home the basket was filled with washing and back in the kitchen the boiler, which had cooked the hams, was scoured and filled with dirty clothes.

Cleaning jobs were fitted in between. They were vital because in these better houses clothes were passed on to her, dresses into which she changed every afternoon to await her husband.

JOHN TOVEY: In the grounds of Miller Howe

"He was a chauvinistic drunkard with ideas above his station," recalled John. "But he had style."

By the age of ten John's father had returned from the forces and the young lad was sent off to Nottingham to join his parents.

"It was the biggest trauma of my life. My mother was a cow, the devil incarnate. My father beat me horribly. I used to get back to Barrow whenever I could.

"Nothing was ever said, it wasn't in those days, but my grandmother knew what was happening."

By the age of 16 he could stand home life no longer and applied to the Colonial Office in Rhodesia after seeing an ad in the Daily Telegraph.

Being under the age of consent, he forged his father's signature on his passport and completed plans for departure. His family hadn't an inkling of what was happening.

"I agreed to accompany my aunt to a spiritualist church in Barrow on the Sunday before I was leaving.

"In the middle of the service the medium stopped what he was doing, came over to us and said I was going on an epic journey in the near future.

"He said I would be safe, fit and would flourish. I whispered to my aunt that I was leaving for Rhodesia on Thursday. She had hysterics. I had to take her out of the church."

His lifelong condition of being a workaholic started in Africa. Sixty-hour weeks, night classes for shorthand and typing fitted in.

"I wanted to become a court reporter, but couldn't get my speed up to 160 words a minute. I took it down, but couldn't read it back. It's the only thing I have ever failed at."

He became a private secretary. By the age of 21 he was earning a grand a year, ran a Humber Hawk and had a personal household staff of five.

But, according to John, he was hated by the whites.

"I did too much for the blacks, you see.

"I taught the Africans shorthand, typing and office routine." After five years he became violently ill and was rushed back to the Liverpool Hospital of Tropical Disease, suffering from an infected liver, cerebal malaria and dysentery.

Once recovered, he decided to take leave and refused an order to return immediately because riots had broken out. When he did go back his boss sacked him and transferred him to Ghana. Here he worked as a court clerk, sorting out mining concessions.

It was cushy but boring.

He returned to his roots, to His Majesty's Theatre - later razed to the ground to make way for a corporation car park - and to the happiest days of his life.

His salary for working round the clock, doing everything from loo cleaning to acting (on just one occasion), was peanuts rather than pounds.

John saw the Arts Council grant arrive, the first to be given to a weekly rep company, matched by two other £1,000 cheques.

"We owed £2,800, but instead of paying off our debts we had the whole place refurbished. After that we played to packed houses for two years."

There was never any money. John decided he should get out and try to earn some by persuading the manager of the Old England Hotel, at Bowness, that he needed a private secretary.

"You'll need pin-stripe trousers and tails Tovey," came the command. He pawned his 8mm Kodak to oblige. The suit cost him £2 and the remaining £2 he blew on a meal of pork and chips.

He rose to manager, moved to other establishments as general manager, took himself off on a cookery course to Kendal college and the rest is history.

"It was to the tutor there, Mrs MacFarlane, that I owe so much."

In 1971 he bought what has become one of the most prestigious hotels in the Lake District, Miller Howe, for £26,600.

John spent the first 18 months sleeping in the cellar, using the Bendix washer as a bedside table.

For ten years every penny made was ploughed back into the business and John Tovey's name became synonymous with top quality and gourmet expertise.

He praised a dedicated and long-serving staff for helping him find huge success. You can only ever be as good as they are, he said.

He has written several books. The latest, 'John Tovey's Entertaining on a Plate,' comes out in the autumn to coincide with a new series on BBC Wales.

And the regular Tovey column in the Radio Times is seen by 11 million readers.

John, 58, has other solaces in his life these days - Ozzie his dog and a Rossendale farmhouse complete with swimming pool and test kitchen for television work.

He's anxious to find religion, too. "It is taking some searching out. I can't find a decent vicar," he said.

"Being rich isn't about money," he told me. "It's a spiritual thing and involves a great love of life. And for those reasons I am very rich."

Suzie Hayman: The darker side of life

Published June 25, 1993

THE SOUTH Lakeland country cottage is idyllic, nestling under a hill with a pretty garden. Inside, beams, scrubbed pine and a writing table. The scene could be straight from Beatrix Potter. But there are no Peter Rabbit and Benjamin Bunny plots dreamed up here.

The author has to live with darker threats than those posed by Mr McGregor. Right now she is jittery about a nanny whose employer is sexually abusing her.

SUZIE HAYMAN: Ponders others' problems

And then there are the unwanted pregnancies and desperate suicide attempts. Real life has hit this rustic retreat in a big way.

Isolated it may be, cut off it isn't. For here lives Woman's Own agony aunt Suzie Hayman who, thanks to the fax, puts herself in the firing line for the magazine's four million readers.

Each week she gets around 200 letters. She reads every one and personally answers as many as she can.

This ex-teacher, who quit in disgust at what she says was a total lack of respect her colleagues had for the kids, is one of an elite band of problem page editors.

They meet regularly for lunch in town - London, that is, not Kendal. Ideas are bounced, theories thrashed. And back at work they often contact each other over a tough case.

Today's Virginia Ironside, Chat's Tricia Kreitman, they're good at lending an ear and giving advice. After all, a problem shared....

Suzie follows a strong tradition on Woman's Own. Angela Williams had the job for 29 years. Peggy Makins took the original Evelyn Home pseudonym.

And while Evelyn may have had to grapple with complexities, like how to encourage children to eat their greens, Suzie's letters are more likely to deal with the depths of degradation.

Everything that is nasty, dirty and sinister in society she has to cope with.

No longer is this magazine about knitting patterns and recipes. Its readers range from teenagers to pensioners demanding a diet of real issues with no holds barred.

Suzie reckons she is well equipped to deal with the letters which flood her home. She has worked in family planning and is a trained counsellor.

And while Marj Proops might hate the title agony aunt, Suzie says it sums up the job well. "Aunt suggests someone who cares for you but is one step removed and the pain you get is so amazing that agony is the right description."

Giving advice is not her role. Suzie sees her work as a permission-giver, providing the nudge so readers may sort out their own dilemmas.

Pointing clients in the right direction, involving other agencies, not getting directly involved are hallmarks of the aunts.

"I need to be able to walk out of my workroom at the end of the day so that I can recharge my batteries, go back and help others. Although that is not to say some of my letters don't haunt me.

"I'm very worried about this nanny at the moment. I just hope she's taken my advice and got out."

Accusations that letters are made up are nonsense. No-one could have that sort of imagination, she says, and the hoax problems stand out a mile.

The author of several books on subjects ranging from contraception to foster children, Suzie Hayman takes her job very seriously and says it is one she will stick with for a long time.

Some of the problems may seem trivial - like threats made in chain letters.

But to the victim they are a nightmare and if Suzie and the aunts can throw in sense or solution they have succeeded.

2

Shift on the sands

Cedric Robinson: Guide to the sands

Published October 19, 1990

Autumn is here and most of the visitors have gone. For Cedric Robinson - Sand Pilot and Queen's Guide to the Kent Sands - it has meant an end to this year's hugely successful treks across the Bay.

Everyone said the same thing, even Cedric. The scene looked like a Biblical reconstruction as he led hundreds at a time over the treacherous, unforgiving mud flats euphemistically called Grange Sands.

Not that guiding across the Bay is anything new. The monks of Cartmel Priory were doing it as far back as 1326. It's just that Cedric has turned the walks into a major tourist attraction.

And sadly for him, he can't charge his walkers a penny. Under the terms of the ancient appointment he gets 700-year-old Guides Farm at Kents Bank and a small amount of land for as long as he keeps the job.

The fact that he has turned the role of Guide from being guardian to maybe only 20 walkers on a couple of expeditions a week in 1963 to regular crossings of hundreds at a time, is immaterial.

Appointed by the Queen to Guide, he would like more money but gets his satisfaction from sharing his beloved sands with so many.

CEDRIC ROBINSON: On the Bay he loves

"There's nowhere like it on earth," said Cedric staring across the Bay from his cottage.

"I never wake up and think I can't face the sands today, they're always different. Every morning of my life I get up, look through the curtains and never see the same thing twice. The scene is constantly changing."

Cedric has never been abroad, he doesn't want to go. He's left the region only twice - once for a brass band concert in London, the other when he was called up for National Service.

"It was hard, the southerners were very difficult to mix with. I met a man from Preston, though. He was all right but then we got separated.

"My father was the same. He went to war, saw lots of places, came back and never wanted to leave again."

He, like Cedric, was a Flookburgh fisherman. They trawled with horse and cart, then tractor and trailor. In those days there was a reasonable living to be had from shrimps, fluke and cockles.

Times changed, the fishing industry went into decline, Cedric and another fisherman found themselves jobs in a Barrow factory.

"The heat and noise were terrible, we worked in vests and carpet slippers. We stuck it out for a fortnight."

So when in 1963 he was made Queen's Guide to the Sands he was a very happy man.

Not that the job is a doddle. Far from it.

On each walk he is responsible for the lives of every man, woman and child in a bay notoriously lethal with quicksand, savage currents, strange tide patterns which have claimed around 150 victims over the years.

On Cedric's four-mile walks from Arnside to Grange he says he takes away the risks.

He deals with hidden dangers and marks the route with laurel branches, which will keep their leaves in all weather conditions.

"When you are a fisherman you take chances. You stay out as long as you can when you are fishing or cockling, but with walks it is different. They have to be completely safe.

"The only problem is with numbers. I do try to limit them but when I arrive at Arnside and see extra crowds I can't blow my whistle and say only those who have booked can come."

Cedric is cagey about how many he actually takes across at any one time, officially it's around 200, but there have been many more on occasions.

"I know the route and adjust to however many walkers we have. I often have to cross the river twice."

The river is just another of the Bay's obstacles yet, despite having to wade knee- to thigh-high in the cold water, it rarely puts potential trekkers off.

The elderly and young tackle it as part of the adventure. And adventure it is.

"Most will have never done anything like this before. It is the experience of a lifetime," said Cedric.

He has become something of a celebrity and as long as it doesn't involve leaving Grange he is happy to appear on television, be interviewed for radio, be featured in newspapers and magazines.

"I like working with TV crews because they get as much from the Bay as I do.

"Most haven't been to the area before although I suppose they will have been abroad and they come from cities. They see this and they can't get over it."

Cedric has written four books, popular and good money-spinners they are, too. Naturally they are all about the sands and his work on them.

He has even had a pub in nearby Allithwaite named after him - Guide Over the Sands.

His wife, Olive, gives unstinting help and support.

She illustrates his books, deals with bookings and telephone calls.

"It is very much a partnership and I couldn't do the job without her," said Cedric.

Their daughter, Jean, had shown signs of following in dad's footsteps, she loved the sands, spent hours on them.

But she's living in Wales now with a young family so the chances of another Robinson becoming a guide are very slim.

The lethal, severe but amazingly beautiful 120 square mile stretch of Morecambe Bay holds no fear for Cedric.

Yet last year he found out what it was like to be panic stricken.

He suffered a detached retina and feared his sight would be lost, along with his job. The prospect of never being able to see the sands again filled him with dread.

Thankfully an operation was successful, although he can no longer walk far without wearing dark glasses.

As well as being Guide he is also coastguard and has had to deal with the Bay's few fatalities.

Fortunately most who venture on to the sands treat them with respect. Those who don't have been taken quickly.

"I've seen a tractor disappear without trace in 10 minutes in the quicksands. Now we have modern rescue equipment, people can be brought out safely and quickly, if we can get to them before the tide."

In the old days it made sense to take horses and carriages over the sands to Morecambe, Lancaster and Arnside. It was double the distance by road.

"Bodies used to be taken over for burial. One carriage got stuck in the quicksands and the coffin went into the river. That particular body would have ended up not in Lancaster but probably in the Isle of Man."

Changing tide patterns saw the crossings virtually disappear and then came the railways. Cedric has developed his own form of transport in the Bay - a tractor with a specially adapted trailer, complete with cushions, so the beauty of the Bay can be seen without walking

"It's been really popular. I want to put Perspex sides on so I can take visitors out in all weathers."

And that might be a good business enterprise, for this is a service for which Cedric can charge!

With an honorary doctorate from Preston Polytechnic to his credit, his other claims to fame are giving A.J.P. Taylor a piggy back over the sands and riding over them with the Duke of Edinburgh in horse and carriage.

"I am 57 now and God willing I will be able to carry on for many, many more years.

"There will be somebody ready to step into my shoes. There has to be. The sands can never be without a guide."

Jack Manning: On the Wet Sahara

Published May 31, 1989

The slimy, austere sands of Morecambe Bay are as grotesque as they are beautiful. They are menacing, dangerous, yet to the men whose families for generations have fished the murky waters, they are a parody of paradise.

The so-called Wet Sahara is mean, demanding and right now threatening the livelihoods of the few remaining Flookburgh fishermen.

Victim to pollution and modern man's excesses, the Bay can no longer give adequate supplies of shrimps, fluke and cockles.

Each fishing trip produces a meagre catch. A bad season has been followed by a disastrous one and without a miracle of nature, the fishermen know the end is in sight.

King of the sands Jack Manning, like generations before him, has spent his life catching fish. At 56 he knows he will not be able to carry on until he retires and is looking for other work. But thoughts of the old tractors, trailers and nets becoming museum pieces fill him with deep sadness.

He has seen other fishing communities die, losing their heart and soul to become pretty tourist villages.

His one consolation is that he flatly refused to allow his son to follow in his footsteps, for Jack saw the writing on the wall 15 years ago.

"I knew I was going to be the last generation, but thought I might just be able to see my time out. It looks as if I am not going to make it," he said.

"Making a living from full-time fishing is virtually impossible.

"It sounds like a sob story - it is a sob story, but I am not pleading poverty at all.

"We can manage on savings. But it is the decline of fishing which really gets me down."

And the thoughts of no longer spending great chunks of his life in the often cold, bleak Bay dismay him.

Even to a complete stranger the sands have a magical attraction. They have claimed lives, caused enormous distress, but to the fishermen they are like nowhere else on earth.

Jack's life on them has been filled with experiences. He's seen the good times, when pickings and takings were high and the tragedies....they once almost killed him.

He started fishing before tractors were used, competing with as many as 30 other horses and carts in one small channel.

This year there are only four men left, the odd tractor looking incongruous and lost in the huge, wet area.

"Through the 50s and 60s we made a good living. When I left school in '49 factory and manual workers were on about £8 a week I could make £20 or more.

"If you could make £1,000 it was a hell of a thing. I was making it."

But the tide has turned in more than one way and now Jack is lucky to pull in more than £10 a day.

JACK MANNING: On his fishing way

"I have to look to get out of fishing, but it is hard when you are my age and have no recognised skills."

Until eight years ago Jack was in the estuary twice a day, virtually every day; summer winter; day and night.

Night-time autumn shrimp catches were almost legendary; for some inexplicable reason it is now impossible to fish for them in darkness.

They disappear.

"The Irish Sea is a dustbin. We have Heysham nuclear power station and Sellafield.

"Glaxo, which is probably environmentally conscious, had a spillage of sulphuric acid recently, but will not be prosecuted.

"If we stepped out of line and caught salmon illegally the water authority would jump on us." Jack said he had been taken to court a few times for 'offences relating to salmon,' but not for a few years.

"I made the mistake of appearing before the Bench in my best suit. Others had gone in work clothes and were fined £10. My suit cost me £50."

Despite pollution, Jack said Flookburgh fish, as far as he knew, had never made anyone ill.

Certainly the demand is there - it is the supply that has dried up.

For, despite enormous effort, sometimes in the most atrocious weather conditions, a good catch now is worth only a few pounds.

When photographer Mike Barker and I went on an early morning fish with Jack he said it was the best haul for days. At the end of the day, sorted and peeled, it netted only seven or eight pounds of shrimps and 15lb of flukes.

We had been out more than four and a half hours. It would take an hour for each pound of shrimps to be picked and the flukes had to be filleted.

Shrimps sell for £3.60 a pound and filleted flukes for 80p a pound.

JACK MANNING: Pulling in his nets

At one time there was so much fish coming into the village a co-operative was set up with 20 workers to deal with the catches.

Flookburgh Fishermen Limited now has only three full-time employees and unless the autumn produces a good season it will not survive another two years, says Jack.

Cockles were always plentiful, too, and unlike other fish could be found throughout the year.

"There were a good lot of cockles over the past two years, but these foreign fellas came in and took them all," said Jack.

"Up to 250 men, all on the dole, came from Liverpool and North Wales on to our cockle beds and virtually cleared the lot. Nearly 100 tons, several wagonloads, were taken.

"The last time they disappeared in the hard frosts of '62 and '63, it took 15 years for them to come back."

And flukes, which are caught in pre-set nets after the tide's ebb, are also in very short supply.

One of Jack's most vivid memories of life on the sands was when he narrowly escaped drowning in 1976.

With only a few days to go to Christmas it was to be the last fish before festivities got under way.

"The wind in the early hours had been howling like hell from the east, but by 5 o'clock the windows had stopped rattling and I decided to go," he recalls.

Two hours later, as the tide was rushing in, the tractor air-locked and the two minutes needed to free it, not to be had.

Time was running out by the second. Two miles from shore, with skies still as black as night, Jack had no guiding lights.

As he struggled through the freezing water and mud he threw off his clothes, fighting every inch of the way.

He needed to get to the safe side of the channel, but the tide was roaring up it at a terrifying rate. Two thoughts crossed his mind.

His father Harold had died earlier in the year and he thought it ironical he would probably fast be joining him and cursed the fact he was still carrying keys to his garage, boathouse and car. He should have left them at home!

Whether it was luck, supreme fitness or the sheer will to live which got him through is diffcult to say.

But that particular trip not only nearly cost him his life. His tractor, nets, clothes, oil-skins and catch all went.

He was £1,000 poorer that Christmas. But as least Jack was still around to tell the tale.

As a schoolboy he rescued a young evacuee girl from the quicksands, but was unable to pull out her foster father. He perished.

Treated with respect the sands, to those who know them, do not present too many hazards. The greatest risks seem to be from expecting them to provide full-time work.

"In the past it has been swings and roundabouts, with a bad season followed by a good. When you get a succession of bad, it becomes serious," said Jack.

"For heaven's sake don't make it all gloom.

"I have enjoyed my life fishing. To be down here on good days is like nothing else and if I had my time over again I would do the same thing."

He says his greatest pleasure in life is to bring his young grandchildren down to the sands to fish.

Knowing they can never become full-time fishermen with yards full of nets, rusty old tractors and character must, as Jack would say, hurt like hell.

* **SINCE** this piece was published Jack Manning's only son, Stephen, has left his job as an engineer with Barrow shipbuilders VSEL to fish the Bay full time.

3

Head in the clouds - feet on the ground

Arthur Evans: In love with nature

Published November 9, 1990

'I could write this myself - I would just say Arthur Evans is a genius and leave it at that.' Blue eyes laugh at you from a face which looks like a weather-beaten russet apple. In fact Arthur Evans is a lot of things - teacher, writer, historian, naturalist and joker.

He writes the Westmorland Gazette nature notes every week, contributes to other publications, dispels the myth that naturalists are as dry and lifeless as autumn leaves.

But Arthur Evans has to be a one off. The dictionary describes a genius as a person with exceptional ability of a highly original kind. And that seems to sum up our Arthur.

For his great grasp of nature and history is coupled with a razor-sharp sense of humour which searches for the funny side of just about every situation.

It made him a big hit with the Ulverston kids he taught, wrecked his propects of joining the profession's hierarchy.

Because in teaching, like writing, he wanted to make his subject come alive, to be appealing to everyone and he wasn't going to kowtow to the establishment to do it.

When pupils were being introduced to D.H. Lawrence's 'Snake,' Arthur waltzed into a colleague's classroom with a live, giant boa constrictor wrapped round his neck.

ARTHUR EVANS: Wanted to make his subjects come alive

32

"She nearly screamed the place down, but I wanted to show the kids snakes weren't slimy and horrible but beautiful, warm and very powerful things.

"I loved teaching. I had a fantastic rapport with the kids. Every morning I had flowers on my desk, until I discovered they had come from the cemetery."

A Furness man born and bred, Arthur left Barrow Grammar School with no formal qualifications and has spent the rest of his life regretting it.

He joined the Post Office as messenger boy. It had advantages. He was able to get on board ships harboured in the town, meet the captains.

By the time he was 17 and war broke out he was in Whitehaven, pushing himself to the limits sorting out mail and lecturing troops in his spare time on aircraft recognition.

"I was full of bullshit in those days, but I had a photographic memory, although looking back I don't know how I had the cheek to do it."

He was desperate to get into the Navy. He had always been fascinated by ships but was turned down on medical grounds. His heart was said to be weak.

The shift work at Glaxo which followed bored him to tears, but he still had his books and an insatiable thirst for history and nature knowledge.

By then he also had a wife, Jean.

"I was fed up with work and Jean asked whether I was man or mouse. That made me make up my mind to try writing for a living.

"It was a harsh winter that year. Travelling was difficult and I couldn't make enough to keep us."

Eventually he landed a job at the shipyard looking after ships' plans and was able to carry on writing.

Two books followed. One sold around 4,000 copies, the other - Naturalists' Lake District - was 10 years ahead of its time according to Arthur....and flopped.

He met a man who had been to teacher training college as a mature student and Arthur thought it sounded a good idea. So he took himself off to the college at Chorley where he qualified as a teacher.

Jean also trained at the same time.

"Coming out of industry I found teaching very strange. It seemed pedantic and pompous.

"My contemporaries from college became headmasters and couldn't understand why I didn't. I was always too much my own man.

"I loved trying to teach poetry, especially to the boys. They were terrified of appearing to be puffs or sweeties by showing a liking for language.

"We produced word pictures, it didn't matter if they didn't rhyme."

Now pushing 68, Arthur retired at 63.

He's still apprehensive going into Ulverston pubs on his own. There's always a clamour of old pupils wanting to buy him drinks.

And with time on his hands, Arthur turned to his first love, writing.

"I suppose it's a bit like teaching a form of communication. I like to think I'm helping people to wake up to what they've got around them.

"People think naturalists are going to be pedantic and are going to lecture them. Life is too short for that.

"I can't say I'm a one off but I do like people and I like to pull their legs."

He has a rare talent for chatting up old ladies.

"It makes them feel 10ft tall when you whistle at them and say 'Hello gorgeous.' So many are lonely and loneliness is a terrible thing."

Birds - old, young, feathered or otherwise - attract his attention.

It's all part of his love of life, people, animals and nature.

I spent a truly memorable day with Arthur and Jean, learning a lot about flora, fauna and history. Not always easy when your stomach aches from excessive laughter.

They took me on the Tebay road stopping at Boroughbridge, with its fine farm and Roman history.

Here, remains of a fort are buried beneath Friesian pasture, the bath houses covered and forgotten.

We saw the Lunesdale Gap road, built by the Romans who marched in legions of 5,000 men over its long, exposed stretch.

Further round there's Gallows or Gibbet Hill at Carling Ghyll and that's where the body of notorious Smurthwaite was left to rot.

"They were a bad lot.

"They used to roam the road as highwaymen and thieves.

"They used to hang people at Appleby or Lancaster and hang them up there as a deterrent to others.

"Carling Ghyll farm was owned by the chief warden of the Tower of London, but I think he did sweet bugger all in reality.

"In this one, tiny area there is so much to see.

"Round the corner is Borrowdale; the Tebay Borrowdale, that is.

"The Roman Road there led all the way to Watercrook in Kendal. In parts it was 21ft wide - an M-road."

We walked up a short way, saw a buzzard resting in a tree, gathered handfuls of sphagnum.

"You know sphagnum?" asked Arthur.

I didn't.

"It is an antiseptic moss which absorbs water and lives in acid conditions.

"It was used as a dressing in the first war, just like it was used in prehistoric times.

"It was used by Eskimos for nappies, too.

"This would have been a busy place once, important cross roads.

"Drainage pipes were made from Alston lead.

"Did you know a lot of the pipes in Rome were made from Alston lead?" I didn't.

I finished the day wiser. I'd learned a bit about the Romans, seen birds I hadn't heard of, like the fieldfares or Norwegian thrushes, just in for the winter season.

And I found a friend. Thanks for a terrific day, Arthur!

Peggy Braithwaite: Keeper of the light

Published November 12, 1993

WHEN they were leaving Diana alone they targeted me instead, groaned Britain's only woman lighthouse keeper. And by making the remote, wild southern tip of Walney Island into a media mecca, Peggy Braithwaite coins it in.

Not for herself, though. Before consenting to an interview she demands a minimum £20 fee and every penny goes into the lifeboat fund.

A lifetime watching and protecting shipping in the treacherous mouth of Morecambe Bay has made her all too aware of the perils of the sea.

An answer to a journalist's prayer she might be, but her rise to fame has left her unmoved.

"It's not because of who I am, it's where I am. I am just a normal person doing an unusual job."

Blunt, straight and down to earth, she is unaffected by camera crews from both sides of the Atlantic and a continual clamour for interviews.

Fun for Peggy is tramping out with her spaniels, gun in hand.

Since her family moved from Piel Island in five boats when she was five, Walney lighthouse has been her world.

And as retirement approaches next year she faces what will probably be the greatest challenge of her life - adjusting to living in a bungalow in Barrow.

"I can't very well lean out of my window and shoot rabbits there, can I?" she sighs.

Her age is a matter for the War Office and Indians and is no-one else's business, she says. When she climbs down the lighthouse's 91 steps for the last time she will be ending her family's long links with the building.

Her father and sister before her were keepers. Peggy took over in 1975.

Erected in 1789 to guide sugar and slave traders from the West Indies round the Furness peninsula and into Glasson Dock, it has given her a privileged, if hard, life.

Her first job of the day is to switch off the beam, as bright as 460,000 candles - at sunrise. In June that could be 4.30 am, in winter a much more acceptable 8.30.

"If it's a rotten day I'll go back to bed. If I feel like staying up I will do some painting or cleaning."

The pristine buildings and yard around the lighthouse gleam with paint and polish. Peggy says her assistant, Ian Clark, is even fussier than she is.

She tramps up the long, stone spiral to her high-rise world with dustpan and brush in hand. Every step is swept and at the top she takes up a duster and polishes the copper-backed reflectors.

It was during the war that she and her sister were first faced with painting the 75ft high tower. The lighthouse had to be camouflaged and a firm was sent along to do the job. The foreman said he was too old, another refused to go up.

"In the end, father said: 'Never mind, my two girls will do it.' He always did ignore the fact he had two daughters. That's probably why I'm not very lady like."

Suspended on a bosun's chair, the girls carried on with the precarious painting exercise year after year - without incident.

PEGGY BRAITHWAITE: The lady with a lamp

38

The family didn't feel particularly vulnerable during the war. They had 170 men and a battery of guns to protect them and the peninsula.

"I used to be invited by the officer-in-charge to go down to the rifle range and shoot. He thought if a girl was hitting the targets it would make the trainee troops try harder."

Peggy lives at the lighthouse cottage with retired garage manager husband, Ken.

Shunning suggestions of loneliness, she says cities are the loneliest places on earth. Not Walney. Twitchers out bird watching provide conversation if she wants it. Normally she doesn't. Her spaniels are company enough.

Holidays have been few and far between.

"If I'd wanted them I'd have had them. I've been to London and as soon as I've seen gulls on the Thames I have come straight back."

Times have changed in the lighthouse. Technology has made life easier.

No longer does Peggy have to climb the tower three times a day to wind up two hundredweights of lead clockwork by hand. Now there is an optic drive motor, electricity and two standby generators.

Once, when a switch failed late on a Saturday night, pint-sized Peggy pushed the light round by hand using a stopwatch.

Eight years ago she got the BEM from Princess Margaret who was visiting Holker Hall. She couldn't hear what was being said because a jet passed at a crucial moment.

Anyway, she was just another in a whole line of celebrities who have met and presumably been bowled over by this remarkable little woman.

4

Sins of the flesh

Frank Stainton: Disciple of wine

Published November 23, 1990

He became the wine disciple of Cumbria - respected, revered, followed to the far corners of the county. Single-handed he took on the old-boy establishment, dispelled the myths and mystery of the wine trade, showed the ordinary man and woman there was more to life than plonk.

Frank Stainton was, and is, the wine merchant of the people.

And how could the guy who created spoof magician character The Great Franko - an incongruous mixture of Italian and Westmerian - have been anything else?

By making audiences laugh he got them to look beyond the likes of Blue Nun to find delights from the world's vineyards and at the same time built up a very impressive business for himself.

He's just celebrated his 45th birthday and has temporarily retired from public life. If he hadn't, Frank says, he'd have never reached 46.

When he started his own business in 1984 his wine talks had already taken off in a big way. In the first three years he hurled himself around the county, hosting 400 wine evenings, using different characters and huge amounts of energy.

"They became a cult, but the stress and strain of starting the business and being out three or four times a week, often driving quite a long way, nearly killed me.

FRANK STAINTON: A taste for wine

"They were a marvellous way to introduce people to new wines and of advertising my business, but in the end they were a hazard to my health."

And so the funny man, who as a fat nine-year-old had already mastered the art of entertaining and went on to raise thousands of pounds for charity with his unique brand of humour, bowed out of the limelight.

"Maybe I'll go back to it when I've more time and not working 100 hours a week in the business. I'd like to do more writing, too, and perhaps another television slot - one day."

As a Castle Street School boy, 'Fatty Stainton' was top of the Christmas show bill with his magic act.

By the early 70s The Great Franko had emerged, poking fun at magic in his weird Westmerian/Italian accent.

It took Frank ages to come up with the right character. He tried many. The thick Lancashire lad in a flat cap didn't work; neither did the Germanic Herr Frank, he was much too formal and serious.

Franko was a riot, adored by all who saw him. Tragically, he has now been laid to rest, forever.

"If I brought him out once more, word would get out and I'd be inundated with requests. People ring me three and four times a week as it is to give talks," said Frank.

The Stainton saga of wine evenings began in 1964 after Kendal soroptimists asked Frank to talk about a trip to Alsace. He was with Kendal wine merchants Youdells at the time.

"They were a stoical bunch of ladies and for 40 minutes I blinded them with science.

"Then I started doing evenings at the Brewery Arts Centre, Kendal, and it slowly dawned it would be nice if the audience laughed."

And that's how it all started.

Frank would introduce a country's wines using a character with the right accent. As wine markets opened up in the States and Australia his scope broadened.

Anecdotes from his wide experience in the trade were embellished and embroidered until he had a devoted band of followers.

He seized on funny stories; couldn't believe his luck when the Aussies first hit the world market with brand names Kangarouge and Wallaby White.

And then there was the exchange with Mme Bollinger. The champagne Bollinger, naturally.

"Frank, I drink champagne when I'm happy, when I am sad. Sometimes I drink it when I am alone; when I have company I consider it obligatory. I trifle with it when I am not hungry, drink it when I am. Otherwise, Frank, I never touch it, unless I am thirsty."

Louis Roederer, the French wine king, offered his smart French house to Frank, a Glaswegian and a Birmingham merchant.

"The fridge was stuffed full of champagne and we were told our host would be very upset if we didn't use it all during our stay.

"The Glaswegian said, 'Don't worry about that, pal,' and kept us up drinking it until four in the morning, saying 'Open another bottle, we canna let the Froggies down.'

"The Brum was slaughtered on our last night. We got him on the plane and he was comatosed.

"Half way across the Channel he opened a bleary, bloodshot eye and said: 'Frank, I've got this funny floating feeling'."

Westmerian farmers came in for stick, too. The story of one bringing a bottle back to the shop with less than a half inch of wine left is almost a legend. "Me and t'missus had to be sure it was off, like, before we brought it back."

Sadly, when he was asked to do a weekly slot on Border TV Frank wasn't given a chance to perform, only to present.

"They certainly didn't get the best out of Frank Stainton," mused the great wine seller.

Frank went into the wine business straight after school and spent 21 years with Youdells.

In his early days the industry was a closed shop of snobbery and intrigue.

"Basically, it was full of drop-out public school boys, with dark suits and pomposity, but as it became an immense business the industry attracted different types, clever people, good at marketing and selling techniques."

So 'Fatty Stainton' isn't an oddball any more. He's not fat either, having just shed three stones. The battle with the bulge is constant, though.

"My weight has varied from 11 and a half stone to 19 stone. It was a struggle doing those 400 wine evenings and having supper at them all. Well! I couldn't offend the little old ladies who had served them for me, could I?

"I suppose if I am to be remembered, I would like to think it would be for being the people's wine merchant. The pleasure of seeing customers walk through the door never ceases. It's a great life in the retail trade."

So, though Franko is dead, Stainton battles on. He gives a couple of wine talks a year and his fans wait in anticipation for the wit, panache and razzmatazz of this raconteur to reappear on the entertaining circuit.

Joy Moore: Chocoholic supreme

Published January 29, 1993

You are what you eat we are told. That being the case Joy Moore should be pig fat, covered in spots, with rotten teeth. For she is a chocoholic. All she eats is chocolate - two pounds a day - and says she's fighting fit and healthy from it.

JOY MOORE: Feeding her addiction

46

She wears a size 14, has skin the likes of Elizabeth Arden would kill for, no dental disasters and says she never ails a thing.

Unlike most addicts Joy doesn't have to crave. She can indulge any time she likes. Joy's dependence on cocoa led her to open the 1657 Chocolate Shop in Kendal.

And if she is on a binge staff have trouble keeping up with her. As soon as shelves are filled with the delicious mouth-watering confections Joy has a crush on, she eats them.

On these days she comes before the customer. And the next day she takes it easy by eating plain chocolate as opposed to fancy, filled delicacies.

But now she faces a problem. Her doctor has ordered a rest. From work, not chocolate.

Since starting her business four and a half years ago she has hardly stopped - working seven-day weeks, often 18-hour days, seldom taking a break.

Visitors seek her out from all over the world. She gives talks, makes chocolate masterpieces for top businesses and creates three-tier wedding wonders.

On GP advice she's off to India where there'll be no curry for her. Joy hopes the solid bars of couvature - a top-quality cooking chocolate - she will be taking with her survive the humidity and heat.

Only during Lent does she deviate from her bizarre diet. And she suffers.

"I get the shakes. It's far worse than giving up smoking. And food, which needs preparing and cleaning up after, gets stuck in my teeth.

"I eat all the time. I don't have meals and never get constipated. It suits my lifestyle."

Now chocolate is a well-known aphrodisiac. Madame du Barry is said to have given it to her lovers. Casanova drank it instead of champagne. Monks in the seventeenth century were warned it was a violent inflamer of passion.

Joy confesses she doesn't get any kicks from it.

Her strange eating habits started while she was teaching in prisons. She was unable to take meals at normal times and found food dried and revolting by the time she had chance to eat it.

"I started snacking on chocolate because you could eat it any time and is sold everywhere.

"I never feel hungry any more or fall faint on the floor. I just grab a bar of chocolate. It is a way of life."

The only thing chocolate deprives her of is vitamin C, she says. And that she can have supplemented.

Husband Brian has a bit of a marzipan fetish but otherwise eats normally and daughter Amber lives too far away to make 1657 chocolate her staple diet.

As for Joy, she has 193 varieties to go at and 26 different drinks. There is just one thing she is not likely to touch and that is an exquisite Lilliput model of the Chocolate Shop, a kilo of solid chocolate.

These are going to be sold as a regular line at around £16 a time. Rather an expensive nibble, even for Joy.

* **A DIETICIAN** said that Joy's eating habits were not to be recommended.

Women aged between 19 and 50 need around 2,000 calories a day. Joy's two pounds of chocolate add up to 5,000.

Although she will have adequate supplies of calcium, protein and iron, the problems start when you work out the fat content, said the expert.

A normal diet should include 30 per cent of fat. Joy's chocolate represents more than 50 per cent.

And with deficiencies in fibre, B and D vitamins and zinc, Joy could find herself at risk from a range of illnesses like heart disease, gall stones and serious bowel disorders.

5

Rural rebels

Chris Trippear: Glass fibre genius

Published July 23, 1993

To the man in the street Chris Trippear is a champion. To civil servants, local government, the Inland Revenue and insurance companies he is a grumbling appendix. In lulls between storms this 47-year-old Shap inventor quietly gets on with his latest creation. His genius hinges on turning simple ideas into sensational products - in glass fibre.

His fake seventeenth century four-poster beds are placed in stately homes. The unwitting public pay to see them.

His look-alike Lakeland slate roofs are now on some prominent Lake District buildings - with the taunt to planners to spot them, if they can.

And Trippear's latest bucking the system brainchild is a crofter's cottage - on wheels - capable of being split up when its inhabitants decide to go their separate ways.

Two fires and a flood have wiped out Chris's operation on three occasions. In the latest incident, a crisis was made out of his drama which took insurers five years to settle.

A large sign detailing the saga stands prominently on his barn. The £18,000 compensation he was originally offered would not have built a lavatory, he said in terms rather more basic.

He held out and got the quarter of a million he needed to rebuild the ruined farmstead. And the notice stays up for every

CHRIS TRIPPEAR: Crofter's cottage on wheels

day he had to wait, despite a plea from the insurance company to remove it.

When I went to see Chris he was on the phone to a woman from waste disposal. He is in-filling his land to protect it from future flooding.

As usual he had to get a bit stroppy and demand a site meeting. Pity, he said, she had such a nice name.

"I always have to take the bull by the horns and bugger bureaucracy because, like the law, it is an ass and common sense and logic have to prevail."

A boat-builder by trade Chris has, over the years, developed a unique talent for putting glass fibre to seemingly bizarre uses. His gift is in stoking up immediate demand for his products.

"A mate had installed a seventeenth century four-poster in the back of his cattle truck. It was a great bird-puller, but it tipped in a dyke on the Isle of Arran and he asked me to repair it."

Chris took a mould and started what turned out to be a decade of decadence with his £1,500 Jacobean copies going to the States, Hong Kong, the Middle East.

Drews, the London interior decorators, asked for a king-sized version to be sent to Nigeria - for our Queen and Duke to sleep on during a state visit.

"I thought it was going to be my big chance and I could be By Appointment to the Queen, but there was a military coup a fortnight before the tour and the trip was cancelled."

Features in glossies like Homes and Gardens were his transport to success.

"Seven or eight stately homes wanted one and I was ordered on oath not to say anything because folks had paid good money to look at them. You have got to have honour among thieves."

The first recession killed trade and after dabbling with fitting-out inns in fake oak panelling he changed tack completely.

Chris came up with chill rooms, 20ft or 30ft sealed units for abattoirs or food preparation.

And hitting on temperature retention he turned tables again and used the same techniques, first for flat roofs and then his ultimate brainchildren - chalets and slate roofs.

Mr Glass Fibre is about to demolish the temporary home he has had planning wrangles over, move the crofter's cottage out of his workshop on to his land and install himself in it.

"Just until I replace my ruined house," he stressed.

This mobile home comes complete with conservatory, storage loft and its insulation means that even in the dead of winter, heating costs won't spiral to more than £5 a week.

It is going to cost around £25,000 for a Trippear cottage on wheels.

They are capable of having extensions and being split up as demand dictates.

Chris thinks they could become the council houses of the 90s and are perfect for mobile workforces.

"When someone changes their job they don't need the hassle of selling and buying houses.

"With this they can move it with them on the back of a lorry."

Even though the creation is in its infancy there have been inquiries from holiday operators in Spain and Russia. Although Chris says they will have to think of something better to pay with than roubles.

His 'slate' roofs have also hit a hospitable market.

"I could never understand why men went up ladders carrying three tons of slates when you could make look-alikes in long sheets."

And while the price of materials is the same, the fitting costs tumble with glass fibre copies at only 50p a square foot.

A planner's nightmare has become a home owner's dream - roofs on the cheap and, as yet, not one discovered by local authorities.

And that is where we leave him, contemplating his next venture - the new house - and the brushes with authority it will inevitably bring.

"I don't go out to buck the system. I'm just trying to get some sense into it and if I have one aim it is to get the word 'civil' back into 'servant'!"

* **SINCE** this piece was published the Lake District Special Planning Board has discovered a Trippear plastic roof section - on Muncaster Castle.

Bob Orrell: A lifetime adventuring
Published October 30, 1992

Lake District writer and broadcaster Bob Orrell has a B allergy. Bureaucrats, bank managers, the banal and boring make this craggy and controversial rolling stone rebel. Since the age of nine, when he ran away from his parents for the first time, Bob has shunned convention like a contagious disease.

At 57 he has no money, no hope of making any, no chance of comfortable, cosseted retirement.

What he has, though, is a life-time of adventure. And while his task these days is to drag farmers from lethargy in a regularly contentious countryside column, the real potential must be in a biography.

Bob Orrell said it would be a diary of a waster, a rise to obscurity. Yet few could have encountered such rich pickings along the way.

His career spans lighthouse keeping to millionaire's yacht skipper; RAF mountain rescue team member to working with world famous Texan oil rig firefighter Red Adair; and always a writer.

BOB ORRELL: Through the Lakes by packhorse (Picture: Ivor Nicholas, Workington)

Frustrated by his unwordly poet and musician father, Bob first tried to sever family ties on holiday in Blackpool, when he set off in a rubber dinghy to sail the world.

Lytham lifeboat crew put an untimely finish to that expedition but the nine-year-old was undaunted.

The following year he hitched a lift from his native Manchester to the Isle of Skye.

He was sent to live with relations in Shropshire, where he was a step nearer his consuming ambition to farm. It wasn't long before he got the wanderlust again.

This time, at 14, he stowed away in a Fleetwood trawler, was discovered and hauled before a furious captain who handed him over to police in the Isle of Man.

Undeterred, young Bob tried again. This time the boat was off the north coast of Scotland before he was found and taken to the skipper. It was the same angry man.

"He said they were too far out to head back with me, so I went with them to Iceland spending three atrocious weeks fishing in foul weather.

"I got £20 and a bag of fish at the end of it."

Bob won a scholarship to a Shropshire agricultural college. But settling down was never going to be Bob's scene.

Instead he ran away again, back to the Isle of Skye, where he lived in a cave in Glen Brittle with an earl's daughter. The nobleman was not amused and sent police to collect the girl.

By then Bob had become a keen climber and decided the RAF mountain rescue could benefit from his service.

He also lied his way into the brass band, claiming skills on the B-flat bass. Performances later, when it was discovered he couldn't play a note, his penance was to play the bass drum.

A nasty incident followed when the instrument broke free from his supporting strap and rolled towards a group of dignitaries. Band duties came to a sharp halt.

There were no notable rescues either, but the RAF did introduce Bob to a very special girl.

BOB ORRELL: A writer in silhouette (Picture: Ivor Nicholas, Workington)

"If there is such an animal as a perfect woman, she was it."

She shared Bob's love of adventure and was kidnapped in Morocco, where she was travelling alone, by a gang of white slavers. She managed to escape, but was caught and shot.

In his devastation, Bob went to the Hebrides where he became lighthouse keeper on the Butt of Lewis.

He moved on to Ardnamurchan Point, upset authorities by complaining of Dickensian conditions, committed the cardinal sin of falling asleep on watch and allowing the light to stop revolving. He was out.

His time as a deer stalker was fairly uneventful but when Bob became a hospital porter in Hampshire he was fired for inciting nurses to strike.

He then rekindled his ambition to sail the world, but the vessel he bought wasn't even capable of being towed on land without dropping to bits.

"The next port of call was the Lake District, lowering the tone of Brathay where I became the only non-public school member of staff."

Naturally that didn't last long, but he managed to put in two years at Wray Castle where he was in charge of administration, seamanship and, amazingly, discipline.

What followed was a job any fellow would give his right hand for - instructing at the first girls' outward bound school in Wales.

"The idea was to mould the characters of seventy 17- to 20-year-olds. It was a hell of a strain on mine! The school motto was 'Serve, shine not to yield.' The principal said I was an evil influence."

A collection of jobs followed - running a sailing school on Windermere; climbing and guiding in Langdale; boat building.

He finally thought he had struck it lucky when a millionaire asked him to skipper his yacht in the Mediterranean.

Even that didn't last. The bourgeois and Bob were an oil-and-water cocktail.

The next Orrell instalment was one of the most dramatic and from it he produced 'Blow Out,' the only non-fiction book to chronicle life on an oil rig.

He tells of the horrors of the Hewett A disaster, which he witnessed first hand. He was working as a radio operator in 1968 when the rig suffered a disastrous blow out.

Helicopters and lifeboats fought against gale-force winds and raging seas to evacute men from the gas-filled platform. Three workers perished.

When Red Adair was called in to cap Hewett A, Bob went with him to man communications.

"Red got half a million. I got £10. And that was stopped out of my wages the following month."

That harrowing experience was followed by lobster fishing at Ravenglass then a spell in business making farm gates and horse jumps. Another of Bob's financial disasters.

Instead of worrying himself into an early grave Bob took to the old packhorse routes of the Lake District, on fell ponies. Expeditions to the Highlands and Isle of Man followed, along with four books.

He lives in Ennerdale, where he offers bed and breakfast to keep the wolf from his door.

6

Keeping them in the fold

Katy Cropper: A celebrity doghandler

Published September 28, 1990

Champion Hawes sheepdog handler Katy Cropper has joined the media circus and unwittingly become a celebrity. Her victory in BBC TV's One Man and his Dog contest opened the floodgates for eager producers and keen feature writers to latch on to her vivacious personality, striking good looks.

In the past month she has appeared in just about every national newspaper, had her face beamed on to television screens across the country.

Inexplicably The Sun has given her a miss.

Otherwise it has been a Rat Pack encounter *en masse* for 29-year-old Katy.

Some have been provocative, others sympathetic, all have produced stunning pictures.

She is, after all, a photographer's dream.

Katy's problem has been with journalists taking her too literally, reporting everything she has said.

And it has landed her in hot water.

"I'm a joker.

"I probably laughingly said the BBC should change the name of the series and the whole thing was blown up out of all proportion in one paper.

KATY CROPPER: Good with ducks, too

64

"I was made out to be a hardened feminist, which I'm not."

Jesting comments about TV commentator Phil Drabble being guilty of sexism were mountains made from molehills, embarrassed Katy and sent ripples of resentment in some circles.

Even the Duchess of Devonshire, who presented the One Man and his Dog trophy, wrote in one publication that Katy was being a bit naughty.

"People who know me know all that has been published is not true.

"I'm not a bloomin' feminist. I'm crazy, but very, very easy going."

Offers of television appearances are still coming in. She drove her six Aylesbury ducks to London in a trailer - yes, she trains ducks, too - to take part in Blue Peter.

While I was with her she had a phone call asking if she would join in a panel discussion on the difficulties women have in doing well in a man's world.

The prospect of appearing with one of the country's leading gay activists and others committed to women's rights did not appeal.

This ex-public schoolgirl, who shunned a degree course in interior design to work in a zoo, knows what she wants from life and goes for it.

After her first encounter with a sheepdog trial at Anglesey, she was smitten, decided to train as a handler and took herself off on an Agriculture Training Board course.

Attracted by the competition, it took her back to school days when she ran 1,500 metres and got through to the Welsh championship finals.

She met a talented handler, Jim Cropper from Rossendale, accepted his offer to move north and married him.

"He taught me everything I know. There was method in my madness! We're divorced now, but still the best of friends.

"I'm going to write a book called 'I Came a Cropper'."

She is unattached right now.

Her ex-boyfriend read in one of those 'terrible reports' that Katy was about to give him the boot and was not very pleased. "That particular reporter was a friend of a friend. I never thought she would write down everything I was telling her.

"I always bounce back and I suppose that might make some people a bit jealous of me.

"I'm very happy, love what I'm doing, am slightly crazy and appear to get away with murder."

In the conventional, established circle of doghandling Katy has to be seen as an oddball.

But she has made a lot of good friends, proved her ability to even the most sceptical and does not care about an odd snide remark.

"Life is too short to worry about what some people might be saying about you.

"I'm in handling to do my best, run my dogs, enjoy it and win if I can."

From her idyllic cottage in the tiny hamlet of Sedbusk, overlooking the Hawes valley, she has set up a business training sheepdogs. She runs Agriculture Training Board courses, demonstrates all over the country.

A couple of weeks ago she was invited to Belfast to take some ducks through their routines - they go through little yellow gates and over bridges.

"They hadn't had their wings clipped and disappeared into the crowd. The dogs had great difficulty finding them.

"Two ended up in Liberty making a terrible mess of the carpet."

Katy's own prize-winning dogs - Trim, a five-year old bitch, and Max, three-and-half - are living proof of her ability and dedication.

She hopes her youngsters Queenie and Roger prove competent, for her sights set on the International Handling Championship were dashed at the Aldwick contest a couple of weeks ago.

As a member of the English team she was up against the best. Her dogs did well, Katy tried hard but minor mistakes cost her the title.

Next year could well be a different story and if the championship still eludes her it will not be for want of effort and perseverence, just bad luck.

Olive Clarke: Selfless service

Published May 22, 1992

The woman who describes herself as a professional retirer, had one more act of justice to mete out. Her job as magistrate and prison parole reviewer had come to an end. Yet, on Olive Clarke's own doorstep, a great wrong had been committed.

A young cob had the audacity to fly in to join the Clarkes' two magnificent swans, which had been especially imported from Berwick-on-Tweed.

Cad that he was, he not only beat up faithful old Porgy, but overnight became toyboy to impressionable pen, Bess.

"It outraged my moral and judicial sentiments," stormed Mrs Clarke.

And she had the accused swiftly removed from her pond to Derwent Water, courtesy of the RSPCA.

Retribution had been swift.

It was how she liked to operate when dealing with juveniles at Kendal court.

A lashing from Olive Clarke's tongue put many an errant youngster back on the rails.

And, in time, they were grateful.

OLIVE CLARKE: Feet firmly on the ground

"It gave me great pleasure when a grown-up man stopped me in the street and said, 'Remember me?'

"He then introduced me to his wife and children, even the baby in the pram.

" 'I never came back,' he said, 'after the telling off you gave me'."

Obligatory retirement at 70 followed 32 years' service as a magistrate.

She had been deputy chairman of Kendal and Lonsdale Bench, chairman of juvenile court.

As a girl this Preston Patrick farmer's daughter spent considerable time developing trout-tickling skills.

And, in later years, when young defendants appeared before her for doing the self same thing, she was constantly irritated.

"Because they did it so badly. I could have shown them how to do it properly."

"The moral behind the story is simple: 'There but for the grace of God, go I.'

"It should be engraved in tablets of stone in every court and in the hearts and minds of every magistrate.

"I shall never know of my court successes, but the failures did come back to haunt.

"This may help you," said Olive.

I'm allowed to call her Olive, she says, because I have known her for a long time.

And she handed me her CV.

The list shows a lifetime's commitment to public service where she has reached the top of many a committee ladder. Her sound sense, judgement, forthright manner, constantly sought after.

As she retires from one thing, she is immediately snapped up for something else.

"I am a professional retirer although retirement for me is a non-starter.

"But then, I am a workaholic."

Her two daughters wanted to organise a 70th birthday party. In true Thatcher style - yes, there are many similarities - she declined.

"Dears," she retorted, "father and I have to attend a meeting in Hull that night."

Her other current withdrawal is from Durham prison where she has been deputy chairman of the board of visitors and on the review committee for parole.

One of the country's toughest jails, in her 25 years she came up against hard, bad, men and women, where, she said, emotion could never play any part in assessment.

One old timer, with an arm-long list of previous convictions, pleaded his case to get out early.

"I can't stand it in here any longer Miss, they're not my class," he implored.

"I'm a straight burglar; I've never knocked down old women."

"It demonstrated to me that in all walks of life there are professionals," said the woman who was made an MBE for her services to Cumbria in 1979.

In her 70 years Olive Clarke has had just two homes. Both in Preston Patrick.

She moved into her beautiful Georgian farmhouse after her marriage 45 years ago and says she has lived happily ever after.

Husband Arthur, a farmer, has been her rock. Her family of two daughters and four grandchildren, her great delight.

Her work for WI, which she joined at 15, has seen service on many national committees. For a decade she was county chairman for Westmorland.

In that time barely a week went by without her picture, hatted, of course, appearing in the Westmorland Gazette.

"I don't mind the jam and Jerusalem jibes. Jam, after all, is about home making and I strongly believe we all build our own Jerusalems, on own home ground and in our lives."

Being brought up in the austere 30s was tough, unyielding and good for character building.

When Olive Clarke left Kendal High she was given a card saying any university would be proud to have her.

But there wasn't enough money to send her. Instead life completed her education, experience her teacher, with a constant stream of graduations.

As chairman of the Transport Users Consultative Committee for the North West, she met regularly with high-ranking ministers.

She also chaired the region's public 16-day hearing for the proposed closure of the Settle-Carlisle line, with 25,000 objectors to accommodate.

This was done by holding sittings from 10 in the morning until 10.30 at night.

A furtive hand one evening shoved a note in front of the chairman. It said could Mrs Smith speak next because she had to get back to Blencow for bingo at seven.

A vital contribution, perhaps, in the eventual victory.

The Clarkes' prized watercolour of Ribblehead viaduct is a reminder of the event.

Mrs Clarke has also been a commissioner of Income Tax, a lifelong supporter of Young Farmers, chairman and president of Westmorland and Furness County Landowners Association.

She says one of her greatest honours came when she was invited to be the first woman president for Westmorland County Show.

She has since been made a life member and still organises the schools' tent.

A Socialist by nature, but a Conservative to achieve what she believes in, her brush with politics came when she won a Kendal by-election seat on Cumbria County Council.

She didn't stand for re-election because of other commitments.

Health service duties, boards of governors - she retired from Endmoor village school only after it got its new building - village committees....the list was, and is, endless.

In everything she has ever done her husband Arthur has backed her to the hilt. Together they enjoy travelling and once their girls had grown up, set off on a camping expedition around Europe.

They regularly go off with a picnic to find new roads in the countryside they cherish.

The old adage from her father - "Keep your eyes on the stars, my girl, and your feet firmly on the ground" - has held her in good stead.

If she could chose herself an epitaph it would modestly say: "She did what she could."

7

Getting to grips with trialing and trailing

Linda Topham: Teenage wrestler

Published April 19, 1991

The ancient and skilful art of Cumberland and Westmorland wrestling is about to see new combat. This isn't a matter of crossclicks, hype, hank and strokes though. This contest is a skirmish over sexes. Should girls be allowed to fight?

It is a question forced out into the open at the Wrestling Association's annual meeting and one with which the powers-that-be are now grappling.

Opinion is divided. Inside clicks - sorry, cliques - think the sport has gone well enough since the Romans introduced it, without being hampered by fair maidens.

Radicals, on the other hand, think a ban on girls would be preposterous; a retrograde step for wrestling; and an insult to female followers.

The situation is as tricky as a cross buttock throw, but not as easily resolved.

Some say they've only got the best interests of the girls at heart. It's a rough sport with plenty of chest work.

What an excuse, exclaimed the father of Linda Topham, the petite Blackpool wrestling teenager who seems to have set the cat among the pigeons.

A Great Britain under-19 judo representative, 17-year-old Linda is a good Cumberland and Westmorland fighter.

LINDA TOPHAM: Getting to grips with the boys

76

Very good.

"There was never any problem when the lads were throwing her all over the place and beating her easily. The problem comes now that she is winning," said Colin Topham.

"I can't believe the powers-that-be are considering banning girls and hope that this is all a storm in a tea cup."

Linda, 5ft 2ins and weighing just under eight stone, is a committed and talented contestant. She practises the archaic sport six days a week.

"The lads are beaten by her and can't take it. But they should be bigger than that, stand up and say she has done very well," said Mr Topham.

In judo it got to the stage where boys were queueing up to compete with her. She became a challenge. And, her father says, she offers the same potential to wrestling.

"It seems like sour grapes. If a man with a moustache starts winning, will they ban competitors with moustaches?

"Rule One says all contests should be open for free competition to the world. If girls are banned then it will have to say open only to half the world."

Jack Thackeray, an ex-wrestler and now Kendal coach and founder of the town's Cumberland and Westmorland academy, has a different fight on his hands.

He says the future of the sport is at risk and is calling for a ban on girls' wrestling.

"I have spent 40-odd years persuading lads to come into the sport. They need all the encouragement they can get.

"Some youngsters take it up never expecting they will have to wrestle girls.

"I'm not a male chauvinist and I have nothing but admiration for some of these girls. The last thing I would want to do is to belittle them, but we have a Catch 22 situation.

"Lads come into wrestling, we train them up and they go off to competitions that might involve a 150-mile trip. They've turned out to find they might have to wrestle a girl.

"If she beats them they are a laughing stock and don't get any encouragement for their effort.

"There is a lot of hassle and it doesn't do the image of the sport any good at all."

Mr Thackeray said if there were plenty of female followers there would be no real complications, they could fight each other. It is because there are so few, they have to compete with the boys.

He said when girls had turned up at the Kendal academy they had received nothing but encouragement, had never been refused entry in open competition.

"That's not to say I haven't had reservations. It only needs a big, tough lad to go to town on one of them and they could really get hurt."

Moves have been made to press for Olympic and Commonwealth Games recognition.

Mr Thackeray said there wouldn't be an earthly chance of ever being included if the sport had mixed competition.

"All this came up because it was felt good lads were disappearing from the scene after losing to a girl," explained Mr Roger Robson, club leader of the Carlisle academy.

"I take a very *laissez faire* attitude, but I do think if the boys can't take being beaten by a girl it is tough. They should get out of the sport."

But Mr Bob Clarke, the Grayrigg president of the Wrestling Association, is adamant that this is not a suitable activity for the fair sex.

"They come in as girls, but don't keep it up. Besides, it is very dangerous as they get older. There's a lot of chest work."

Wife Dorothy, first woman member of the governing board, agreed: "What good do girls do for the sport?" she said. "No good at all."

Glenis Hodgson, 20, from Dent, was typical of most girl wrestlers. She started to fight because her brother egged her on.

"I borrowed his costume and started doing the local events when I was 12. Some of the lads were savage. They didn't want to be beaten by a lass."

With a few wins, seconds and thirds under her belt, Glenis ducked out when she started work.

"There wasn't time to carry on then but if girls want to wrestle with the boys they should be allowed to. A ban would be very sexist."

Barbara Prudham - she's a Raven now, married and mother of three - was a talented fighter from the age of 14 to 16.

She got a mixed reception but no-one ever refused her a fight.

"I can see both sides of this argument," she said. "If there were plenty of girls there would be no difficulty, they could fight each other.

"I got a lot of pleasure from wrestling, it was something different and it would be a shame to ban girls from competing."

Along with Linda Topham, Joe Thelfall is a member of the St Michael's-on-Wyre academy and is a bit of an expert on Cumberland and Westmorland wrestling.

He did a thesis on it for his sport degree and finds the situation absurd.

"Any proposal to ban women is preposterous," he said. "As a club we are totally opposed.

"It would be a retrograde step for the sport and an insult to the females involved.

"If boys feel distressed at losing to a girl, if it is such an insult to them, they should train harder.

"I have competed with girls. My sister is two years older than me and often beat me. She was bigger and stronger. But I never gave up."

The Westmorland Gazette's own Dennis Aris, himself a judo black belt, has been an enthusiastic follower of wrestling for nearly 20 years.

"Girls have been successfully integrated into judo, they fight the boys at club level and are segregated for competition.

"The boys' mothers embroider their trunks during the winter. So they are naturally hardened when they are wearing them!"

Now the future of girls dressing up in the traditional white long johns, vest and ornately decorated velvet pants to compete with the best of them, is in the balance.

The sport, which in its heyday had national appeal, attracting thousands of spectators, even in London, has been through peaks and troughs in its long history.

In 1851, 10,000 flocked to Ulverston for the world championship where the two finalists battled it out for the princely sum of 300 guineas.

"If Cumberland and Westmorland wrestling is going to carry on being appealing, women can do the sport nothing but good," said Mr Thelfall.

Maybe it's hype, possibly it's hypocrisy, but it seems this particular pain in the cross buttock looks set to continue.

Robin Jager: A blasting driver

Published October 16, 1992

They came from all over the country to a bleak Cumbrian hillside, men who would be boys for the day. These are Britain's trial drivers, the poor relations of motor sport. But what they lack in sophisticated cars and glitzy image, they make up for in just about everything else.

Around 25 of these mean machines had been towed to a disused quarry at Forest Head, high above Brampton, to battle it out in what was a national championship round.

I had been coerced to passenger for former national champion and ex-pat South Lakelander, Robin Jager.

He's been involved with the sport for more than 30 years and is said to have made more comebacks than Frank Sinatra.

For he, like all the other competitors, is smitten. It is not just the skill in getting up a series of steep, poled courses - some gradients are one-in-one - but the camaraderie.

"It must be the only motor sport where your closest rival would be the first one to help you if something went wrong," said Mark Vaughan, who had travelled from Northern Ireland to take part.

Seeing the terrain and the motors, which seemed to offer scant protection to riders, I thought it was going to be one of my more foolhardy decisions, risking life and limb.

In fact, according to Robin who lives in Worcester, trials driving is only dangerous if there is a novice at the wheel.

"There has been the odd broken collar bone and arm, nothing serious. Even then it has been down to driver's brain fade."

He is 51 now, affectionately known as Uncle Robin because of the number of 'nieces' he turns up with to passenger him and, he says, he will carry on until he drops.

Charles Pollard, from Lincolnshire, is 73 and has been on the trial trail for 36 years, travelling the length and breadth of the country to compete.

"It is a very satisfying sport, very competitive and, at the same time, very friendly.

"There are no great costs involved, virtually no sponsorship and prizes are trophies."

One driver reckoned you could pick up a trials car for as little as £1,000.

Robin thinks you would have to pay a bit more for a reasonable machine. His is an up-market version for which he shelled out £6,500.

With a Triumph Acclaim 1340cc engine, two-speed gearbox and the all-embracing fiddle brakes, it hasn't yet managed to reintroduce Robin to championship stakes. He hasn't clinched top honour since 1975.

And with me as passenger his chances in this year's contest are slimmer than ever.

ROBIN JAGER: In action at Forest Head

For the rider is supposed to provide potentially vital back-up, leaning out of the car at 180 degrees to help stabilise it on bad bends and to embark on a series of startling, jerking movements when the need arises.

My kids told me I was pathetic, but Robin carried on trickling and blasting for all he was worth.

These are the two main techniques.

You trickle in dry conditions, with wheels rolling rather than spinning. If it is wet and muddy, then you blast your way to the top.

To give huge grip, back tyres are taken down to only two pounds per square inch and the fiddle brakes allow drivers to control each back wheel independently.

Every climb is marked with 12 numbered sub-sections.

The aim is a 0 score. That means you have to get to the top without hitting a post or rolling backwards. We completed 36 climbs in all.

Chairman of the Cumbria Phoenix Club, Mr Gerald Hepplewhite, explained it was the last motor sport not to have grown out of all proportion.

"It is still within reach of motorists. You can get a car from around £1,000, pay a £10 entrance fee and along with a can of petrol, have a great day.

"It isn't a well-known sport and people often confuse it with a driving type test, going up and down banks, but in fact there is a lot of skill in it."

The governing body is the British Trials and Rally Drivers Association and every competitor's dream is to take the BTRDA's top honour, the gold star.

Mark Vaughan makes it across the Irish Sea as often as he can afford, about three times a year.

He's been competing for 15 years and said the Cumbria course was bleak, but tremendous.

He had barely time to acknowledge his win before racing off to Stranraer to catch the ferry home.

The rest of the crowd hung around while results were given and the banter was as swift as the competition had been.

We finished twelfth.

The afternoon had been much better than the morning's efforts, but the placing was disappointing.

A social mix: On the hound trail

Published July 8, 1994

IN A SUMMER bereft of hot days this had been a scorcher and taxidermist Simon Wilson was sweating cobs as he came off the Kentmere fells. For the past hour and half he had been laying a trail around the crags and hills that surround the valley they say is earth's nearest thing to heaven.

The hounds were already arriving. Transported in a convoy of battered vehicles, driven by trainers and owners hoping this was going to be their lucky night.

The peace was shattered. No-one was going to notice the lengthening shadows on the picture-postcard scenery this still evening.

Bookies jostled for space. Hamburger and fish and chip sellers manoeuvered to a key selling position. Farmer, coalman, policeman out to see their dogs run. And to enjoy the crack.

This might be poor man's horse racing, despite an MP and lawyers taking more than a passive interest. Michael Jopling owns a hound. The legal contingent name their dogs Duty Solicitor and Expeditiously.

Hound trailing, say the trailers, is more than a sport, it's an addiction.

Something born in you, that you feel obliged to follow.

Chairman of Westmorland area, Barry Laidler has a posh car - and no dogs.

That way he can be impartial. His crucial role is to video the race end.

After rumpus and tiffs spanning five generations, fracas on the finishing line are now easily resolved.

"There were dirty tricks once," confessed Windermere book-maker Barry.

"In the 50s you could win £5 at a trail and your wage was £3 a week.

"It was a living then. It's an expensive hobby now. No-one is in it for money any more."

Kentmere's top race offered £25. To be divided by six. First got half, second half again and so it went on.

Winnings are sometimes left uncollected.

Tradition rules.

The two men who set the ten mile course are given plastic containers holding aniseed diluted with paraffin, sealed with red wax by the dispensing chemist.

Strands of wool blanket are soaked in the solution and dragged around the rugged hills and vales, over drystone walls. Each man takes half the route.

"Brilliant! It's absolutely brilliant," grinned Coventry burger vendor John Payne.

He operates outside Aston Villa and Birmingham City soccer grounds with his fleet of four fast food trailers, makes enough money to head back to the Lakes every two or three weeks to follow the trails.

He's a Crufts winner of Norwich terriers, but is hooked on hounds. He hasn't got any himself, yet.

"One day, though. When I live here. If only I could persuade the wife.

STEPHANIE STAINTON: A new generation owner

"I always try to get to Kentmere. If God made a Heaven it is this valley and every time I drive up it tears run down my cheeks."

Johnny Matterson shares the passion. If not the sentiment. With five dogs at Kentmere, not much smaller than himself, the Ravenglass farmer said his 30 years' trailing had been well spent.

"Only because he gets in everywhere for half price," laughed Barry Laidler.

This time of year sees the trailers out most nights, bar Fridays and Sundays. Come changes in Sabbath betting laws and that will change, said Barry.

Senior race favourite Valentine won again. It had been worth Sandy Crowe's trek over from Wasdale. He has had 46 years in the sport, says he loves every minute.

"There have been underhand dealings in the past, but it is not something we talk about."

There has been a big clean-up operation.

On the finishing line at the first race were 18 trainers, 11 of them women.

It used to be male dominated. Not now. Language has been curbed, there is more of a family atmosphere.

In a husband and wife team, the wife does all the work, the husband claims to be the brains.

New generation owner-trainer is Stephanie Stainton, eight, from Windermere. She has her own bitch Bess and along with her sister Laura, 11, was given a pup by a disgruntled owner after it failed to perform well in a race.

"Bess, Bess," she screamed at the finish, amid a deafening chorus of shouts, willing the hounds a fast final furlong.

The crescendo peaks and old plastic ham and paint containers proferred to the panting, exhausted animals.

Their rewards vary. Tripe, venison and beef were on the menu this night.

Accusations of cruelty are quickly quashed.

ON KENTMERE FELLS: 'The hounds were already arriving.'

The hounds are skeletal because they are supremely fit. They run two or three times a week at this time of year and would never tackle the arduous course unless they were happy.

"There are no jockeys on their backs urging them on," said Barry.

Chris Clarke can be out six times a week travelling the Westmorland circuit and beyond. He's a bookie with David Mitchell of Kendal. Fed-up being on the losing end this season.

"I'll maybe take £100; £200 on a very good night. It isn't good tonight, though."

Betting isn't exactly fast and furious. These dogs are well known and favourites usually favour. Although, says Barry, nothing is ever certain.

"Gambling has spoiled it," complained Margaret Wilson, from Barrow. Bowing out at the end of the season after nearly 40 years, she said she has had the best times.

"There is too much hassle now," said the owner of the successful Rosco dogs.

As quickly as it was shattered, peace returned to the valley.

Barking dogs bundled back into cars to disappear up the dust-disturbed track.

Ta-tas were to be shortlived.

There were three trails to choose from the next night, two the evening after that and then the big meet at Askam on Saturday.

No rest in a dog's life!

8

Business or pleasure?

Owen Jones: Swill making tradition

Published October 11, 1991

When Anneka Rice's treasure hunt team landed after each mad mission it was Owen Jones who had to maintain the helicopter. His bosses at Castle Air Charters, Cornwall, were in the film business, their chopper fleet used for television documentaries, advertising.

The work was tough, the pressure tremendous. There were no margins for error.

So Owen decided to swap tools and trade. And instead of working on high-tech, multi-million pound machinery he now makes swill baskets.

Not opting out, points out Owen, more like opting in.

Home is an old Lakeland cottage in the beautiful High Nibthwaite valley, his workshop a woodfilled garage-like building. The only pressures here are financial. Owen, 31, has worked as a night porter to help boost the family income.

Wife Luke, an aircraft radio engineer, has commuted between Nibthwaite and Manchester to work in the three and a half years the family has been in the Lakes.

But there are no regrets.

Owen, who served his apprenticeship as a helicopter engineer in the Army, has found a way of life he adores.

Strange how it all happened.

Almost as if it was meant to be, said Owen.

OWEN JONES: Grateful to have learned

He had been promoted to chief engineer, the Cornish company was short-staffed and Owen found he was working himself into the ground.

"The hours got crazy, it was taking over my life, so we decided to leave."

With their two young children, Toby was only three months old at the time, they set off to travel to New Zealand for six months.

Owen had already been introduced to swills by then. His father-in-law, Don Atkinson, who lived at the Nibthwaite cottage, had started to learn the old craft.

Tragically he was killed in a road accident. But his tutor, John Barker from Grizebeck, found another able student in Owen.

"When we were in New Zealand I made up my mind to come here, get in touch with John Barker and learn how to make swills."

John, who worked in Broughton-in-Furness, is one of the last men around who served their apprenticeship in the swilling industry.

Within six months Owen Jones was in business producing the handleless baskets, helping save the centuries-old tradition from extinction.

There was some freelance helicopter work in Essex when Owen spent two weeks a month mending choppers and two making swills.

"It then became swills full-time.

"In three or four months I might have to find more part-time work. It will never make a brilliant living."

But then there is more to life than money in Owen's book.

He sells his swills for £20. Each one takes about an hour and a half to weave, on top of preparation work.

"Swill making was close to extinction, I now demonstrate the old craft at fairs and shows."

Produced from wafer-thin oak strips, the baskets were produced in huge numbers around South Lakeland at the turn of the century. Potato farmers, fishermen, coal miners all used them.

Each starts life as a coppiced piece of oak. The trunk is then quartered and put into a large cast iron boiler to soften the wood.

This is split into thin strips and the final swill produced by weaving the strips around an oval rim of hazel.

"Some of the old craftsmen take the secrets of their trade to the grave. I am so grateful to John Barker for sharing his skills and giving me this opportunity," said Owen.

Peter Monaghan: In nature's paradise

Published January 31, 1992

If you go down to Silverdale woods today, be sure of a big surprise. The chances are you will hardly believe your eyes. The craggy figure engrossed in ancient skills, hazel hurdle making and charcoal burning, is not an optical illusion. Peter Monaghan is real.

He is a man with a mission. To bring management back into South Lakeland woodlands, which have been sorely neglected since the Second World War.

He wants to stop the decay, protect them for future generations, make them once more a place for wild flowers, butterflies.

And in so doing, raw material for this coppice merchant and other woodmen will be in plentiful supply.

The next step in Peter's campaign is to buy a heavy horse to heave out timber from tricky areas where machinery is a liability.

He has already worked for Holker estate and in woods around Witherslack where he lives. His current contract with the

National Trust is seeing Eaves Wood, in Silverdale, coppiced for the first time in 60 years.

Before the war South Lakeland's woods had more than 1,000 men working in them. They left to fight and never returned to their old jobs, explained Peter.

Without any thinning or management the woods became a tangled mess, plants perished through lack of sunlight, butterflies and wild animals disappeared.

With the hazel Peter takes out he makes hurdle fences, woven strands of split wood between rods, or sails as the old craftsmen called them. In a good day he can make four or five sections. It's labour intensive and slow.

Some of the wood that he can't use for hurdles, he burns down into charcoal. His concession to technology is a portable steel kiln.

And while the old charcoal burners used to stay with their smouldering mounds for ten days, Peter can produce half a ton in two. He spent a night in the woods the other week, tending his kiln.

"Mine is mainly used for barbecues, but in the old days a lot of the charcoal produced around here went into furnaces for gunpowder," he explained.

It may seem an idyllic existence, working in beautiful woods, but Peter gets annoyed when anyone suggests it's a romantic pastime.

"It isn't. Today is a lovely, frosty morning; I would still be here if it was pouring with rain. And it isn't a game. This is a very serious business.

"Forestry is the second oldest profession!"

Without his wife working to help support their two children, Peter, 47, could barely make a living. One day when he can, he hopes to be able to train other foresters to carry on with his work.

He has been to an area in Germany, near Bavaria, to look at how horses can be used in woodlands.

PETER MONAGHAN: Master of an ancient craft

His ambition is to have a German Coldblood alongside him. Small by working horse standards, only about 15 hands, but immensely strong and placid.

Whereas the German government funds these horses, there is no such help for Peter who is having to save hard-earned cash to buy one. But the benefits would be huge.

"'In certain areas machinery is best, but in others horses can work better, bringing timber out of difficult terrain."

Peter said he had read an article about the history of Witherslack in the 1820-30s, saying how many different jobs were supported by the woods.

"Around 16 men were working with timber, making clogs, furniture, candle boxes, wheels, charcoal, coffins, as well as the woodcutter.

"I would like to develop an infrastructure which would create jobs again, even if they were only part time.

"Schools complain about underfunding, but we could supply the material for woodwork classes, fences for farms, timber for small carpentry businesses."

And Peter says with trade opening up in Europe there should be co-operation between countries, so foresters could learn from each other.

Richard Haward, National Trust warden for Silverdale, said Peter would be coppicing three areas during the winter, with volunteers coming in every fortnight to lend a hand.

LUKE - Lune and Kent Estuary's NT support group - has raised money for the project, which has the backing of English Nature.

"I am very excited by the whole thing," said the warden.

Coppicing, or thinning of small trees and bushes, will once more allow sunlight into the woods.

"Soon we will have primroses, cowslips, violets back again, and in turn these plants will attract butterflies. It used to be a brilliant butterfly area."

PETER MONAGHAN: Working the hazel for hurdles

9

When the light goes out

Jane Renouf: A heartbreak tale

Published March 26, 1993

Exactly three years ago Jane Renouf's young son Jimmy curled up in her arms and died. After a 20-month valiant battle against pain and despair that his leukaemia had brought, his tortured little body found peace.

He was eight-years-old. A wiser, braver and more dedicated fighter would be hard to find.

They were qualities he undoubtedly inherited from his mother who bore his illness with amazing courage and Herculean strength.

Not once did Jane lie to him.

When Jimmy realised he was dying they talked it through just as they had everything else.

"Mummy, while you're here my light will never go out," he had told her.

After his death she felt she had betrayed him, powerless to stop it extinguishing.

But within two months she made up her mind to write about Jimmy, his cancer and how her family coped with distressing treatments, drugs, hospital life.

JANE RENOUF: Proud of her Jimmy

JIMMY

No Time to Die

Jane Renouf

And when all that failed, how he was sent home to die with virtually no specialist terminal back up.

'Jimmy No Time To Die' hit bookshops to coincide with the third anniversary of his death.

The aim was to keep his light shining.

The result is an utterly shattering experience for everyone who gets through its pages.

It describes the day-to-day realities of child cancer. There are no hysterics, no accusations.

It tells simply and matter of factly how leukaemia robbed this Ambleside family first of normality and then of their first child.

I was embarrassed asking Jane to sign my copy. Its pages bore the ravages of tears, yoghurt, bubble bath.

It barely left my hands for two days and never left my thoughts.

"Don't worry, a grown man sobbed reading it while travelling on a bus through London," said Jane, who is the Westmorland Gazette reporter for Ambleside.

But much more than that. It is a book of hope, laughter and love, showing how this wonderful family refused to be swamped by sadness.

Even though 150 children die from leukaemia every year, the cure rate now stands at about 70 per cent. As Jane says, Jimmy was one of the unlucky ones.

Reaction to Jimmy's story has already been swift and positive.

The Sir John Fisher Trust has donated £100,000 to Cancer Care at Lancaster for cancer projects, including providing counselling care for children.

And some changes are under way at Pendlebury hospital, in Manchester, where Jimmy was treated. Counselling for families with a dying child is now available.

Ironically, Jane never intended the manuscript should be published.

Writing about the cruel events as they unfolded was her way of letting go.

She had not kept a diary, there was no time. But she found she had perfect recall and could remember everything that happened with total clarity.

For three months after tucking up her two other sons, Martin and Christy, she took herself up to the attic where Jimmy's train set lay gathering dust.

It had been his favourite place and Jane felt he was with her as she wrote into the small hours.

"It became an obsession.

"There was an urgency to write it. Yet I did not want to reach the end because it was like being with Jimmy.

"When I finished it was the final farewell. The funeral was everybody else's.

"This was mine."

Her photographer husband Paul had been right behind her, her tower of strength, as he had been right through the ordeal.

He had cared for younger son Martin and baby Christy, born during Jimmy's illness. His birth brought another seriously sick child into the family.

Christy nearly died as a tiny baby, resulting in slight brain damage which affects his speech and balance. Jane had him with her in Pendlebury as she cared for Jimmy through his gruelling treatments.

Jane's only outright criticism in the book is reserved for the decaying hospital building in which superb staff battled in dreadful conditions to care for seriously sick and dying children.

And within its crumbling walls there is a vast store of research, endless case histories of child leukaemia. They could hold the secrets of causes and prevention.

Jane cherishes a hope one day there will be enough money to investigate them and maybe solve the mysteries of this devastating disease.

Another of her Utopian dreams is for a fully-staffed bone marrow transplant unit at Pendlebury

Only three of its eight beds were functioning when Jimmy was there.

And families still wait around in corridors for hours.

After one bone marrow test under general anaesthetic Jimmy was propped between two chairs. He needed a blood transfusion but it was six hours before a bed could be found.

That was only three months before he died.

A copy of Jane's book is being sent to Health Secretary Virginia Bottomley.

If she reads it, how could she fail to be impressed by its courageous simplicity?

"I do not want people to accuse me of being bitter because my child died.

"Anger plays no part in it. It had to be done in a matter of fact way."

Paul hasn't read 'Jimmy' yet. He finds it too painful.

But he helped edit scripts and is very proud of the book.

As time was running out for Jimmy it became vital to pack in as many wonderful experiences as possible.

He drove a train at 110 miles an hour, flew a light aircraft, travelled to Sweden to meet Father Christmas, became an Army tank commander for a day.

And when quality time petered out, it was replaced by pain, drugs and week upon week of slow dying.

The family relied on Ambleside health centre staff and loyal friends like Karen Gorrigan who turned up daily to help.

The dedicated care and support of the whole community made the last six, bleak weeks bearable.

"It was as if the whole village put its arms around us. Jimmy couldn't have died more peacefully or surrounded by greater love," said Jane.

A percentage from every copy of 'Jimmy' sold will go to the Macmillan fund for home care paediatric cancer nurses.

The beautiful, clever, extrovert Jimmy would have loved the glory.

Through it part of Jimmy will stay alive forever, aged eight, with the knowing face and a slight smile beaming out from the front cover.

"It certainly sorts out the important things. Love and strength and happiness.

"Even in the worst times there was always something to be happy about," said this remarkable mother.

* *Jimmy No Time to Die* is published by Fontana and costs £6.99.

Percy Moorby: Blind man's challenge

Published May 21, 1993

At the age of five, Percy Moorby's mother told him he would end up a blind man. She was right. When he was 44 he entered a world of total blackness. And one which has brought him a life he would be reluctant to swap.

For this hero, who has turned his handicap into an asset, has become a star.

He has judged a beauty contest - by touch; driven a 38-ton truck around a human comb; flown aircraft, looped-the-loop; taken part in stock car races....and won one.

None of it for his own glory, though. Cartmel-born Percy is a modest man. But he'll do just about any stunt for money. Not for himself, for Guide Dogs for the Blind.

His efforts have helped to raise £27,000. That is 27 dogs. And for Percy, who has just had his 60th birthday, it is all about repaying a debt.

"When I lost my sight I was devastated. My wife Laurel went through hell.

"It was only when I got a guide dog that I was able to start to live again.

"I realised someone must have raised money so I could get Josh. They had given me back my freedom and I wanted to put something back," said Percy, who lives in Barrow.

He'd been a fighter from the beginning, never allowing his hereditary *retinitis pigmentosa* to get in the way.

He fobbed off doctors at his medical for the Merchant Navy and spent seven and a half years seeing the world. Russia was one of the few places he didn't get to.

He became plant engineer with a Manchester firm and left only when his disintegrating vision made it dangerous to continue.

But his blindness has given him opportunities he could ever had dreamed of. Adventures which would terrify the sighted.

And when he was asked to judge the Miss Lakeland beauty contest it was Percy who shot to celebrity status, not the winner.

From Sydney to Arizona, the international airwaves were desperate for in-depth interviews. How had he done it? A good grope, or gentle touch?

"I felt hair, face and shoulders. Listened to conversation, got clues about personality," he explained.

"Vital statistics didn't come into it. Although I did try to build up visual pictures of how the girls looked."

Percy's verdict was backed up by his dog, who sniffed around the contestant he had picked. Amazingly all the other judges had independently chosen the same woman, too.

Percy was once asked what he missed most. It was the thrill of driving.

He was introduced to stock car racing in 1985 and gave a cup which he called the Josh Trophy. Last year he won it after a seven-year battle to conquer the course.

He takes his fair share of bangs and bumps and came to grief after his navigator said "That's right," meaning OK.

PERCY MOORBY: Making the most of life with wife Laurel

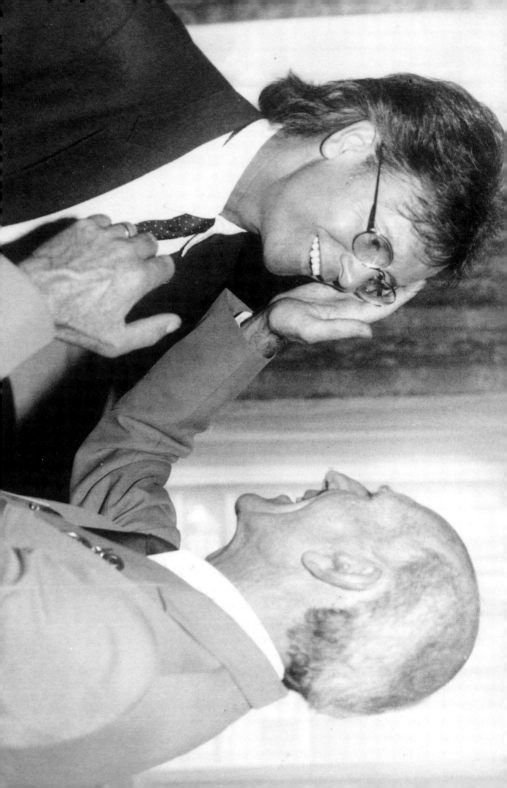

Percy took her literally and smashed two cars.

The eternal optimist applied for a pilot's licence after taking the controls of a glider and light aircraft. After all, he had successfully completed three loop-the-loops, so why not?

The licencing authority was not to be persuaded.

When Percy stepped up into the cab of the 38-ton truck to drive through a human comb, he was alone. Instructions came via radio control.

Only when he was due to take part in a parachute jump did his wife finally put her foot down.

"Laurel said she was not going to push out a blind man in a wheelchair."

Instead, Percy's son did the jump.

Neither of his two children nor his grandchildren have been affected by *retinitis pigmentosa*.

Sailing is one of his great loves. He even skippered a boat in the annual Barrow raft race.

"I have achieved more since I went blind than I ever did as a sighted man. I have never resented what has happened. I have adjusted my life."

A keen gardener, he has even found a way to use his rotavator.

Finding a way is his way of getting by.

"Being blind doesn't mean you are daft; you have to learn to adapt," he said.

"Every day is a bonus to me. I take life as it comes."

And fund raising is going to carry on being an important part of this remarkable man's life. From giving talks to hair-raising feats of courage.

For there is nothing Percy likes better than a challenge.